CAILIN HARGREAVES
@CAYSWORDS_

BE THE LIGHT

WELBECK

Published in 2023 by Welbeck Balance
An imprint of Welbeck Non-Fiction Limited
Part of Welbeck Publishing Group
Offices in: London – 20 Mortimer Street, London W1T 3JW &
Sydney – Level 17, 207 Kent St, Sydney NSW 2000 Australia
www.welbeckpublishing.com

ISBN
978-1-80129-282-5

Typeset by Steve Williams Creative
Printed by Leo Paper Group in Heshan, China

10 9 8 7 6 5 4 3 2 1

For Angel.

You carry the sun inside your heart,

With you, every day feels like summer.

About Cailin

Cailin Hargreaves is a South African-born,
British Instagram poet, artist and politics graduate.
She uses short, contemporary poems and
visuals to discuss themes of personal affliction,
self-healing and growth. Her work encourages
introspection through honesty, accountability
and positivity.

@cayswords_

Contents

Introduction

I share these words with you because they are words
I have said to myself repeatedly; they have lifted me
from darkness and drenched me in their light. They
have comforted me in times of despair, and I hope
they can do the same for you.

If you take anything from this book, I hope it is the
importance of being gentle with yourself. There is
enough heartache, pain and suffering in this world
that you do not need to inflict any more onto yourself.

If you have forgotten how to be gentle with your heart,
or if taking the first step seems unnerving, do not fear.
I hope my words will show you how, and that they will
hold you as they have held me.

My Journey

I remember my tenth birthday very well, surrounded by family, unwrapping my presents, and drowning in all the love I received. Blissfully unaware that in just a few months, my life would be completely turned upside down. In the summer of that year, I developed a virus that wreaked havoc on my body. It began by destroying the cells in my inner ears; I lost all the hearing in my right ear and the majority in my left. Alongside this, I developed ulcerative colitis; an inflammatory bowel disease in which the immune system attacks the lining of the colon, causing chronic pain and ulcers.

I went from gymnastics lessons, piano practice and after-school clubs to doctor's appointments and hospital rooms. I was old enough to understand what was happening to me, and young enough to adapt well to my new reality. I was put on a cocktail of different maintenance drugs, given a shiny new hearing aid (much to my dissatisfaction), and sent back out into the world.

Despite the turbulence and instability that came with navigating an autoimmune disease and fluctuating hearing, I made it through my school years and into the halls of university. In 2017, I graduated with a 2:1 in Politics and International Relations. It was a very significant moment for me, as during my second year I had an operation to insert a cochlear implant into my left ear to help stabilize my hearing. It took me most of the year to recover and adjust to the new sound. So, to graduate despite this, reminded me of my strength and capability.

However, the trauma of facing my mortality and accepting my body's limitations at such a young age followed me into adulthood. I developed anxiety, which started as a small flickering candle but slowly erupted into a forest fire. At first, I kept everything inside, but doing so meant that the small waves of emotions would fester into storms; and when the storms came, they would sweep me off my feet. I began writing to process my thoughts and make sense of my pain. I found a safe space in the words I wrote to lay down my anger, heartache and fears without any feelings of judgement or shame. It allowed me to be the rawest version of myself and unravel the chaos in my mind.

I started posting my words on Instagram and, over the years, my account has grown into a platform that helps uplift and empower people who are going through their own afflictions. Sharing my story encourages others to share theirs too; we sit collectively in our humanity, helping each other to find comfort in knowing we are not alone in our pain. So when a publisher reached out to me to carry this message forward, I was genuinely humbled by the opportunity, and *Be The Light* was officially born.

Unfortunately, while writing this book, I was diagnosed with a second autoimmune disease called primary sclerosing cholangitis (PSC), this time affecting the bile ducts in my liver. The news hit me hard, and I'm still making sense of it as I type these words. This book has given me so much purpose and has shown me that if we dig deep enough, there is always a sense of meaning that can be found in the battles that we face.

As you read this book, I want you to know that I don't have it all figured out; some days, the pain makes a home in me, and on others, it releases me from its grip. I write about my pain openly and honestly to show you that we do not need to give it the power to define us. We can remain soft despite all the ways life tries to harden us.

Sending you lots of love and light. Thank you for being here.

Believe In Your Power

As individuals, we are all unique and hold our own set of skills and attributes. This kind of power is bullet-proof; no one can take it away from us; it lies at our fingertips to use as iron tools.

But, as we journey through life, we forget this power lives inside each of us. We lose ourselves in distractions; we fixate on external things, and change to fit inside the boxes life chains us to. Conformity begins to consume us as we let it strip away our individuality.

Even though this seems daunting, we should not let despair breathe its darkness into us, for we have the strength to stand tall and fight back.

The first step involves inner work and making a consistent effort to understand ourselves more deeply.

It's when we spend less time focusing on the opinions of others, and more time listening to our inner voice, that we gain more confidence in who we are. We stop doubting our abilities and start to live more in line with our purpose. We learn that each of us walks a different path in life, and the ways in which we venture should not be compared; for our pace is always changing, and progress wears us all in different ways.

Therefore, we must bring our eyes back to the road that lies ahead and let our inner voice be the guide so that we can take back our power.

Reflection

Life served me chaos and brought me to my knees. I fell many times yet stumbled to my feet, but even when I picked myself back up again, life always found new ways to strike me down. It would wrap itself round my throat like a choker – dangling its darkness from my neck.

I struggled to catch my breath underneath the weight of each day. As my body lay pressed against the floor, the minutes stretched out into eternity, and the coldness of the gravel filled my mouth with such bitterness that my tastebuds rattled with disgust.

I called out to my courage, but silence filled the air. I started to panic and began rummaging through all the drawers and cupboards of my heart, trying to find it. Only when I ventured down to the depths in me did I discover it there, teary-eyed and half awake, curled up in a ball.

I asked it what it was doing down here, for I needed its strength now more than ever. It struggled to lift its head and answer me; I could see exhaustion plastered across its face, and fear began to pulse through my veins as it looked so weak and withered.

But, I knew it was my turn to be strong, for it had always shouldered most of the burden for me.

I knelt beside it and placed its hand in mine. I squeezed it gently and told it I would not leave until it regained its power.

I admit that defeat washed over me during these moments, and despair filled my lungs. The days lost their colour, and I couldn't find the joy I used to feel from all the little things. Every piece of me was fighting to withstand the chaos life had given me.

However, as time passed, my courage grew stronger, and the more storms we faced, the better we became at weathering them.

I never let go of its hand or let myself be discouraged when it needed time to rest, for it always returned more vigorous than ever. Ready to cough up the darkness and drown me in its light. So, I learnt how to stand in my power and be brave, for the ripples we were making now would soon turn into waves.

you are a beautiful thing

a being dressed in complexity

oozing out in awe

don't let the world make you small

with every ending comes the chance to start again

trust in the power of new beginnings

find yourself once again

return to who you've always been

before life took away your courage

to live authentically

nothing can bury you

if you have the strength to grow

BELIEVE IN YOUR POWER

look at how your strength

held you through your hardest days

look at how the darkness trembled

when you shone your light its way

YOU ARE FIERCELY CAPABLE

you are never alone or powerless

for the force that guides the stars

will take your hand and guide you too

take a minute

to understand your power

from a tiny seed

you have grown into a flower

LOOK HOW FAR YOU'VE COME

when the dark hides your path and you lose your way

the sun will always rise to guide you once again

KEEP PUSHING ON

in the end no one comes to save us

we have to save ourselves

BE YOUR OWN FAIRYTALE

BE THE LIGHT PRODUCTIONS

Title _My Fairytale_

Director _____

Camera _____

Date	Scene	Take

if our confidence is unshakable

the opinions become noise instead of bullets

STAND TALL IN YOUR POWER

words can be vessels of destruction

use their power to lift others up

instead of tearing them down

first the seed lives in the dark

then it blooms and makes its mark

WITH EACH DAY YOU WILL GROW STRONGER

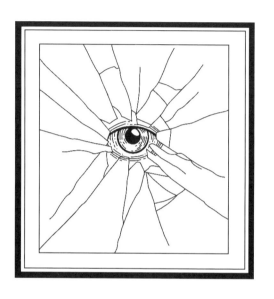

you do not need anyone to love you to feel complete

you do not need anyone to save you from yourself

your liberator is in the mirror staring back at you

the darkest night

always ends in morning light

TAKE COURAGE, FOR THE SUN WILL RISE AGAIN

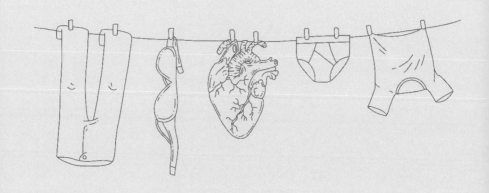

if you clothe yourself with kindness

others will undress their hearts

and wear it too

SOFTNESS IS A SUPERPOWER

kindness is a light shining from the heart

giving others comfort as they navigate the dark

LIFT UP THOSE AROUND YOU

i know it's getting harder now

to fight back the tears

i know it's getting harder now

to overcome your fears

i want you to know

that i've been here before

i want you to know

that there's victory in this war

so hold on a little longer

and your courage will get louder

hold on a little longer

and you'll start to feel your power

though life will always change

let your light remain the same

BURN WILDLY

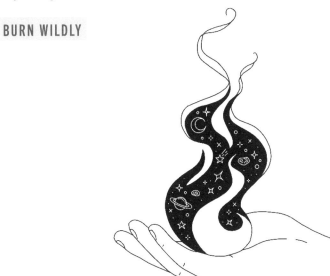

in the remnants of destruction

is the start of your rebirth

PHOENIX

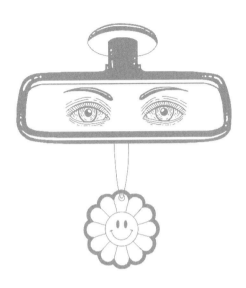

it all begins and ends

with the person in the mirror

FALL IN LOVE WITH WHAT YOU SEE

have the confidence to fill the world

with all of your colours

YOUR COMPLEXITY IS BEAUTIFUL

you were the match

and I the gasoline

you lit a fire in me

that my heart had never seen

AN ODE TO MY STRENGTH

Let Yourself Be Seen

Letting our hearts be seen by others can feel unnerving, and, as a result, we hide parts of ourselves in fear of judgement. This can cause us to become dissatisfied with our lives as we choose to compromise our authenticity for the approval of others.

The cycle of suppressing who we are to control the ways in which we are perceived fills us with affliction, destroying the foundations that we need to live a life built on integrity.

However, when we take a leap of faith and dress ourselves in vulnerability, we allow our relationships and connections to transform and deepen.

When we open up our hearts, we give ourselves space to grow and reach our full potential.

We must make a conscious effort to be true to who we are, to not let the weight of anyone's opinions weigh us down. When we live this way, it becomes easier to meet like-minded people who genuinely care and love us for who we are.

If we stand in confidence and know our worth, we can enter any situation already feeling full and content. In doing so, we don't have to search for scraps of love and acceptance from others because it already exists inside of us.

Reflection

Hello, it's me – the half of you that's trying to be released. All these years of captivity have brought havoc to our brain, and I'm struggling to find the words to explain how you can leave me here to rot inside these prison walls.

We used to be inseparable, like thunder and lightning. I could sit here and write until my fingers become stiff, yet it still wouldn't be enough to describe the intricacy of our connection and how we balanced each other out.

I spoke in flowers, you spoke with fire, and when chaos tried to strip me of my softness, your assertiveness always rescued me. You were my strength when I struggled to be strong, and I was a refuge when you needed tenderness. But as we grew older, we also grew apart.

It's funny how life can change, and familiar things can start to feel so strange. Isn't that what you see me as now – a stranger? A piece of your heart that you've locked away in shame because you fear it will be judged; you fear that it cannot be loved. But there is no shame in sensitivity, or being soft in a world that's constantly trying to harden us.

I know you're just trying to protect me, but hiding half of who we are elicits pain – and I'm not a blemish you can pop or try to squeeze away. I'm not afraid to be seen; I will rattle on these prison bars until I have your attention. As time slips through ours fingers, life accelerates at pace, and I refuse to let us waste any more moments locked inside boxes of conformity, suppressing who we are to gain approval.

I know vulnerability is scary, and unfastening the armour you have strapped to our chest feels unnerving; but when you keep us closed you deny our heart the chance to experience all the joy life has to offer.

So, unlock these chains around my wrists, for you have spent too long making me feel small. It's time you let all the parts of us been seen and lift me from this darkness so we can finally be free.

do not dilute the strength of your love

so that others can swallow it with better ease

THE RIGHT PEOPLE WILL THIRST FOR YOU

KEEP
CLOSED

how strange

that we hide the parts of us

we desperately want to be seen and understood

if you keep reducing yourself for others

there will be nothing left of you

LET YOURSELF BE SEEN

the universe that lives in you

is waiting to burst out in view

REVEAL YOUR LIGHT

open your heart

and let the light flood in

so you can heal from the darkness

that you've grown accustomed to

give your heart the chance to say

all the things it's hidden away

EMBRACE ALL THAT YOU ARE

i decided to unlock the chains

and set myself free

i was tired of being someone

i was never meant to be

my outspokenness

grates against your pride

but i refuse to settle down

i've been silent for too long

THE REVOLUTION

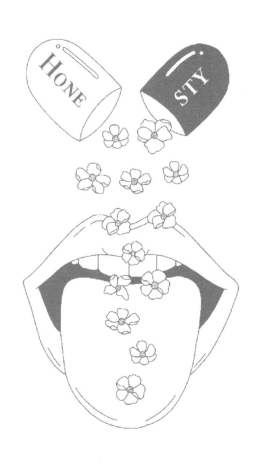

be honest in what you say

the ones who care will always stay

WEAR YOUR TRUTH WITH PRIDE

the beauty of the stars cannot be felt

without a depth of darkness

DO NOT BE ASHAMED OF YOUR SCARS

do not waste time

pretending to be different things

to fit inside spaces too small

for you to spread your wings

the past grew a beast in me

so i set it free

NEW BEGINNINGS

when your give yourself the space

to be who you truly are

what a beautiful thing you will become

AUTHENTICITY IS CAPTIVATING

set your voice free

let it fly out from its cage

for all the words left inside

will fester into rage

All The Words I've Kept Inside

slow down and breathe

there is a missed life waiting for you

outside the walls of chaos

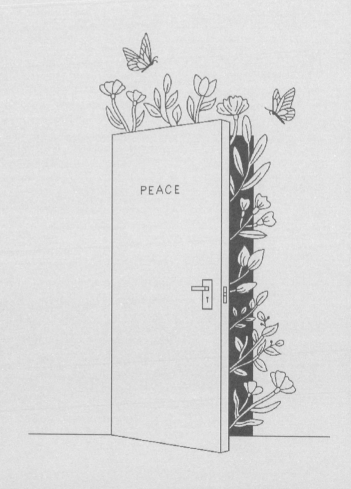

when pride is met with pride

nothing can be solved

when we lower ourselves into vulnerability

we create the right conditions for love to flourish

CHOOSE OPENNESS

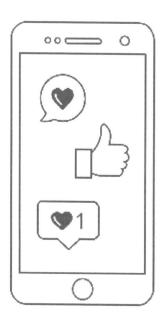

we hide behind our screens

afraid to let the truth be seen

but reality cannot be sealed

behind the filters that we yield

DECEPTION IS DESTRUCTIVE

are you the main character in your story

or have you given others glory?

BE THE AUTHOR OF YOUR DREAMS

i will love you

the way the moon loves the earth

i will give you everything

even when parts of you are missing

A PROMISE TO MYSELF

you have run away

with your thoughts

and made a home inside moments

that are too far away to find

RETURN TO YOURSELF

you will find peace

when you set your heart free

from the prison of conformity

today is calling out your name

it has things it wants to show you

COME HOME TO YOURSELF

You Deserve Happiness

Happiness does not depend on external factors or circumstances; it depends only on you.

Many of us have convinced ourselves that we are unworthy of experiencing true contentment, we think it's something that we have to earn.

However, happiness is at the very core of our experience, and it's in our nature to use it as a tool to evaluate our surroundings, as well as to assess how we feel about life and all its facets.

Therefore, to deny ourselves something that is intrinsically linked to our well-being seems unreasonable.

The obstacles on our path toward happiness are often created by our own hands, as we influence our minds into thinking that it's too elusive a phenomenon to obtain. Yet, when it does arrive, we hold onto it so desperately that we suffocate it before it has a chance to fill us with its light.

We can change this by letting go of the idea that we are undeserving of happiness, as well as releasing the assumptions we have made about how it should look and feel.

In doing this, we take away the pressure we have placed on its back and release it from our expectations, which gives happiness the space it needs to come into our hearts and make a home.

Reflection

I stepped inside the kitchen and tied the strings from my apron round my waist; today, I was going to make a pot of happiness. I've been preparing for this moment for a while, researching extensively, pouring gratitude into everything I did; and practising deep mindfulness.

I had tried to make happiness many times before, but my meticulous weighing and emphasis on following each step of the recipe sucked the satisfaction out of cooking. And happiness always seemed to turn out a little burnt or overcooked when I tried too hard to control it.

So, I decided it was time to give my heart the freedom to experiment and create my own recipe. As I knew happiness was not something that could be easily captured and packaged into a simple set of instructions that applied to everyone. It was far more complex than that, and it tasted different to everyone.

So, I began by taking a deep breath, for my nerves were dancing in my belly. I admit that I was scared, but I knew I was ready. I brought the knife to my hand and began chopping, dicing and mincing all the different flavours and spices together. Next, I cut up all the little joys, the walks in nature and the warmth of love and added them in too.

Once I had finished, I mixed everything together, brought the pot to a boil and covered it tightly with a lid. Now, it was time for me to step back and trust the process, for happiness was not something made in haste. It needed time to simmer and stew, so all the ingredients could release their potency. When it was ready, I lifted the lid and dipped my spoon into the mixture. The room stood in silence as the moment's gravity descended onto my shoulders.

I brought the concoction to my mouth and swirled it around. My eyes lit up instantly! This was it, this was the feeling I had tried to savour all my life. The feeling that tasted like pure joy and deep belly laughs – like someone was hugging me from the inside and warming all the coldness that had settled in my bones.

In that moment, I realized that I no longer needed to go through life as an inexperienced cook following someone else's recipe; I could be the chef of my own happiness, if I dared to follow my heart.

when you detach from the expectations of what could be

the heaviness inside your heart will flee

LET GO SO THAT PEACE CAN FLOW

when you start to notice

all the joy hidden in the small moments

you will see

that happiness is there for you to be

if you do not release yourself from what has gone

how will you hold onto what is coming?

LET GO OF THE THINGS THAT LET YOU GO

in the small moments

where time is unfolding

remember to stay present

and to love the life you're holding

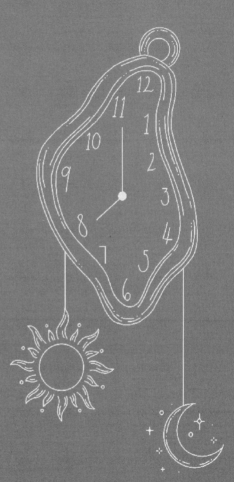

there is no shame in needing softness

if your heart speaks in flowers

A LOVE LANGUAGE

as time passes through my fingers

i am making space for joy

so that happiness can linger

your heart is a tender thing

worthy of the joy that love could bring

TREAT YOURSELF WITH CARE

life will unfold the way it's meant to

regardless of your efforts to control

so don't fight

but let go

and surrender to the   F

                        L

                             O

                                   W

your heart is so heavy because

you hang yesterday on its walls

LET GO, TODAY'S A NEW DAY

how can you enjoy this moment

if you are already searching for the next one?

SLOW DOWN AND BE PRESENT

life doesn't wait for you

you must move forward with it

COLLECT BEAUTIFUL MEMORIES ALONG THE WAY

happiness can bloom in any season

if you choose to water it

INVEST IN YOURSELF

happiness does not enter making noise

it is there every day amid the little joys

LOOK CLOSELY

the world will try

to steal your smile

but let your soul remain a child

adventure seeking

fiercely wild

i'd left parts of me to die

in hidden rooms within my heart

for i was too afraid to walk inside

and heal the hurt that walked the floors

but it was time to make a change

to let myself feel happiness again

so i ventured

d

  o

    w

      n

to depths in me i never knew existed

to open doors and free the pain

that lived within the walls

for i knew if i'd let it stay

it would bind me in its chains

cultivate kindness like it is an art

like there is a spring of joy

pouring from your heart

happiness is a flame

that starts inside the heart

and when you give it space to burn

it swallows up the dark

there is no weakness in letting go

when things become too heavy

for you cannot lift up others

if you have no strength to hold yourself

LET YOUR HEART REST

when the storm settles

and the sun clears the way

give yourself the chance

to bloom once again

as the night welcomes dawn

let the heaviness of yesterday be gone

EACH DAY IS A NEW BEGINNING

kindness is not something

that people need to earn

kindness is a gift you give

expecting nothing in return

with love x

when you arrive at a place

where the solitude does not scare you

settling for less than you deserve is not an option

DO NOT APOLOGIZE IF YOUR HEART WANTS MORE

Healing Old Wounds

Taking the first step toward healing trauma can seem daunting. Wounds of the heart and mind can often go unnoticed — unlike our physical scars, they are harder to distinguish.

Even though we don't see our emotional pain and suffering the same way we see our cuts and bruises, they are there in our awareness, hindering us from our full potential and forcing us to keep repeating old harmful patterns.

But, like physical injury, our emotional pain needs attention, tenderness, love and sufficient time to heal.

We can't change the past and how we've been affected by it, but we can change the power it has over us here in the present.

By having the courage to face our anguish, we become more conscious of our triggers and of how to break out of past affirming cycles that reinforce our pain; our courage helps shift our narrative and heals our old wounds.

Reflection

Hanging from my mind were these perfect scenarios and expectations of how things were meant to unfold and transform into reality. But life was always so explosive and refused to bend to the way I tried to shape it, or stay inside the corners of the rooms I dragged it to.

Life lived in a world of its own, where things ran away too fast for me to catch them, too fast for me to sit them down and tell them not to move.

I tried to scold it, to show life what a mess it made by not behaving. But it was relentless. There was a predetermined fire burning in its belly, one that didn't seem to understand the meaning of negotiation.

When I tried to take control by leading it through hidden alleyways and shortcuts, it would dig its feet into the ground and scream at me in fury. So, I staged a revolution. I tied its hands and feet together and carried it on my back.

But this was exhausting, for I had to stop and put it down to rest so often that I never made it very far. Sometimes it would jump into my throat and climb down into my gut where it would bang things around with such destruction that my body had no choice but to surrender.

I had no choice but to tag along behind it. I was furious at first, to be stuck with such a complicated companion. But life seemed to bloom with happiness once I put down all my weapons.

In the beginning, when the road seemed unending and I thought that we were lost, the worry would wrap itself round me like a skin. Yet life was always certain we were heading in the right direction.

And, after a while, I started to notice that the paths it took me down always had more character than the roads I had chosen. So, I learned to trust life more, even when it brought me to the feet of rugged mountains. For it would hold me close and tell me adventure wasn't for the heartless and, though it may seem scary, it will lift me through the darkness.

i stood at the mirror

there was nothing to see but devastation

and wounds of inner conflict

so i surrendered

i made a stand

i dropped the knives i had in hand

and made peace

with the person staring back at me

come here and lay down

let me wrap your wounds in love

let me dress the pain with tenderness

A LOVE LETTER TO MYSELF

the seed needs to grow before it blooms

so be patient for your time is coming soon

HEALING IS A JOURNEY

i am learning

that i do not need to run through life

trying to find a place where i belong

for when i look within

i am already home

here you are

turning chaos into order

making sense of all the broken pieces

that the pain has left you with

YOU ARE FINALLY HEALING

do not be afraid to reveal the depth of your scars

for no one is a stranger to the weapons that are used

to survive the wars we inflict upon ourselves

BE PROUD OF WHO YOU ARE

i am learning how to let things go

so that my softness has the space to grow

HEALING OLD WOUNDS

if we're too consumed by the ones not meant for us

we'll miss the ones who are

LET THE PAST MOVE PAST YOU

be patient with your heart

it needs time to do the healing

though the pain is heavy now

it's just a temporary feeling

KEEP FIGHTING

i decided to release the pain

so that my heart could learn to love again

BREAKING OLD PATTERNS

there will still be days

when you look in the mirror

and go to war with what you see

healing takes time

be patient with yourself

if you don't let the healing begin

the pain will drown those who wish to love

the pieces that remain of you

the words you say to yourself

are laced with fire

they are spilled to burn through flesh

to cause devastation

WHEN DID THE RAGE REPLACE LOVE?

on some days you will be the sun

growing flowers

on some days you will be the storm

that devours

HEALING ISN'T LINEAR

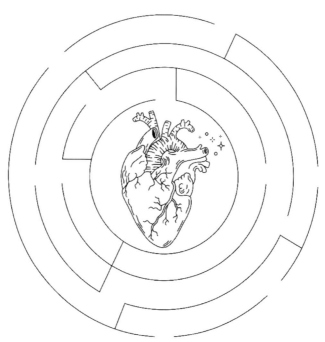

healing is a maze

with many turns along the way

and you will reach dead ends

before you find yourself again

DO NOT BE DISCOURAGED

would we appreciate the sun

with the same intensity

if it were not for the dark

reminding us of its light?

THE NIGHT REVEALS TO US THE STARS

though time has pulled us apart

i am learning how to think of you with joy

rather than the grief that's plagued my heart

healing is a balance

between order and chaos

you must protect your heart

yet let it run wild

EQUILIBRIUM

there is a hardness to me

a tendency toward anger

birthed from pain

birthed from trauma

i try to paint over it with positivity

but the hurt is pouring out from me

frothing from my lips

sticking to my fingertips

i know it's time to heal

so i can hold more than this pain i feel

we are all flowers

searching for the light to help us bloom

BE PATIENT WITH YOUR GROWTH

let the troubles of yesterday melt away

and cleanse yourself in the beauty of today

THIS MOMENT IS ALL WE HAVE

how beautiful

that our heart heals

from the same thing that broke it

LOVE

You Are Enough

The pressure of conformity in society has led us to believe that we must look and behave in a certain way in order to be considered valuable. But how can one standard of beauty be applied to everyone when our traits and characteristics are so diverse? Every person is a complex piece of art, different in design and formation.

No one is perfect, nor were we made to be. Our validation and self-worth does not lie in the perceptions of others.

No merit can be found in comparing pieces of art when they are so contextually different. Yet, society has put physical beauty on such a pedestal that many of us have pinned our worth to our appearance.

There is no denying that beauty can be striking, but if there is no depth behind it, the effect eventually wears off. The magic of our art lies in the ability to make people feel in different ways. Our beauty should be determined by the softness of our hearts and the intangible pieces of light that we give to others, not by what we see when we look in the mirror.

So, on the days when you feel hard to love and a little uneasy, remember that the grandest masterpieces were not flawlessly constructed. Instead, they consist of imperfect fragments of chaos and wonder, which fuse to form something that speaks to the deepest parts of our souls.

You are enough, always.

Reflection

I've been littering my soul for too long, polluting it with heavy words and insults. Being at war with my mind has made it hard to drop the weapons I wield in both hands. Destruction has tattooed itself onto my skin, and its darkness has found its way into my heart.

All these years of blood-stained battles have led to no victor, nor has mercy been displayed. There is nothing to show from all the fighting but a bitterness risen from the turmoil and hardness birthed from suffering.

No matter which direction I look, devastation fills my eyes, for there is nothing to see but casualties and corpses.

Bodies line the street and stretch out into the distance; and seeing such things has filled me with so much torment that my heart has grown ravenous for unity so that there may be an end to this violence.

Bending at the knee feels inconceivable, for I have worn pride so long that it's welded to my chest; but all the warriors in me have grown weary and my body is consumed by pain.

I know the road to peace is treacherous, but it's one I have to take. So, I summon all the courage left inside my heart and slowly begin my journey.

Along the way, I stop to clear the path ahead of me and scatter seeds amid the ruins so that flowers can begin to bloom among the destruction I have sown.

there is no weakness in your need for softness

you are a gentle thing

a delicate being

worthy of the tenderness that your body aches for

inside you lives the freedom

you have searched the world to find

YOU HAVE ALWAYS BEEN ENOUGH

your heart deserves the same kindness

you so easily give to others

BE GENTLE WITH YOURSELF

the depth of your soul

cannot be reached by those afraid to swim

WAIT FOR THE ONES WHO MAKE THE JOURNEY

seeking validation from others will leave you empty

the only person that can fill you up is you

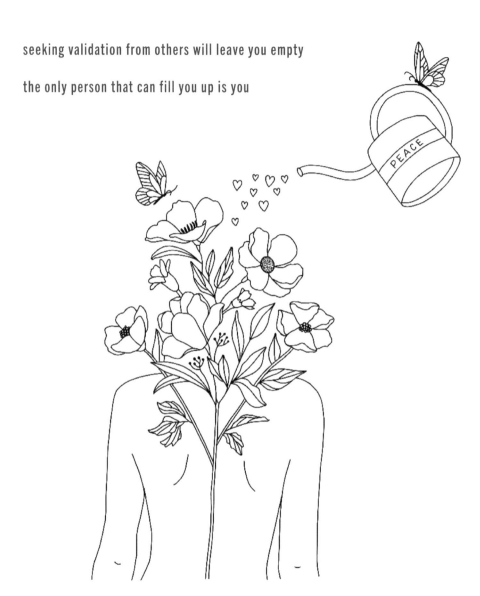

i am learning that this body

is not a battlefield

but a home

to a heart that is worthy of the love it craves

there is nothing to lose

when you choose yourself

to be your own muse

YOU ARE A MASTERPIECE

in the end

when everything is stripped away

all that matters is our capacity to love

and be loved in return

the complexity that fills the universe

can be seen inside your mind

you were made to be diverse

not easily defined

OWN YOUR DIFFERENCES

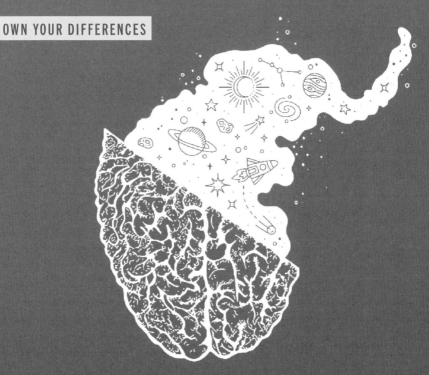

nobody can take away the magic

that lives inside of you

KEEP SHINING

when they return

with promises that seem convincing

remember how they took so much

that parts of you went missing

YOU DESERVE A LOVE THAT STAYS

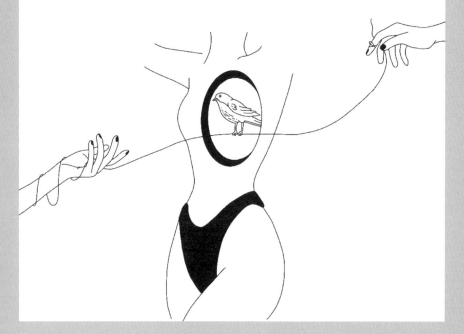

i write about love

hoping it will

p

  o

    u

      r

from these words

and consume you

let it find a way into your heart

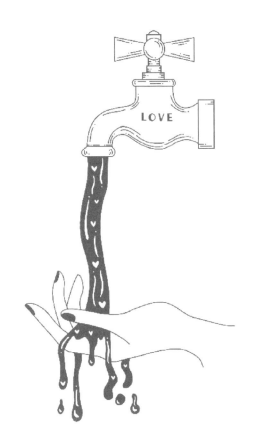

you have spent a lifetime

weaving gentleness through you heart

do not let hands heavy with destruction

destroy your softness

never let anyone make you feel unworthy

you're beautiful in your own sense

and the right person will see that

HOLD YOUR HEAD HIGH

love your faults knowing

that you are a flower growing

GIVE YOURSELF SOME GRACE

in the story of your life

have no fear in turning pages

not everyone will walk with you

through all the different stages

RELEASE THE THINGS YOU HAVE OUTGROWN

water yourself with love

so the seeds in you may grow

SELF-INTIMACY

in the end the only hands

that can hold you up are your own

so make peace with yourself

YOU ARE A HOME

she was a walking poem

a thunderstorm of emotions

demanding to be felt

even when you're at your worst

you still deserve a pair of hands

that hold you up with love

let them be your own

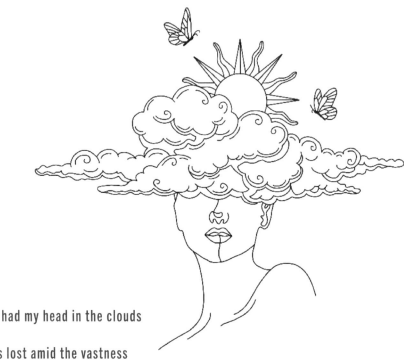

i always had my head in the clouds

thoughts lost amid the vastness

dreaming of a love that engulfed the sky

in such a blaze

that the stars wept with envy

I FOUND THIS LOVE INSIDE OF ME

the only person

that you need to be

good enough for is yourself

KNOW YOUR WORTH, EVEN IF OTHERS DON'T

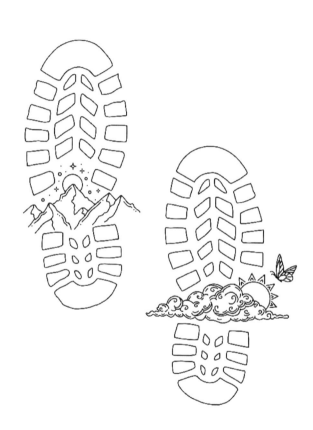

Never Underestimate Your Strength

Throughout our lives we are tested in so many ways — everyone endures periods of suffering. Experiencing challenges is unavoidable, as life brings us all to the feet of rocky mountains and demands that we climb them.

During the ascent, we live through moments of anguish and despair, for there are points along the way that feel more treacherous than others and our fears can start to eat away at us.

Though our softness can begin to harden from the difficulties that we face, we still manage to keep our humanity without letting the darkness destroy us. The strength it takes to do this is undeniable; we need to give ourselves more credit for the courage that we show during these times.

Pain, grief and heartache will inevitably stick to all of us. And when we lay our hearts down to rest, we should not see it as a sign of weakness, rather, as a step that is necessary in order to create the space required for our transformation.

We can only achieve this change through our ability to remain patient, as growth is not something that transpires over night – it takes hours of hard work and dedication.

So, when the clouds start to rain down on us, we should not be discouraged if our courage gets a little lost amid the downpour. For, if we keep our composure and latch onto hope, we will see that, in time, our strength will arrive to hold us through the storm.

Reflection

Nuclear: my strength came to devastate. I saw it approaching in the distance but did not anticipate the speed at which it arrived.

I was completely exposed to its abilities, the weight of my anxiety was no weapon against its calculated compulsion, and neither was the vulnerability it so skillfully withdrew from me.

The worries that plagued my mind were no match for the power that strength radiated and were obliterated by the explosion it rendered.

They burned to dust under a heat that challenged the sun's intensity. Flames tore through my fears, and now they're just a few disintegrated particles floating in the wind – utterly transformed from what they used to be.

They no longer hold the capability to wield power over me as their authority is diminished.

Now, as the dust settles and the floors in me stop shaking, I look around and see the buildings that sheltered my despair lie in ruins at my feet.

 Though the devastation feels insurmountable, and the smell of charred remains pollutes the air, my strength has burned a path to my heart and I can feel seeds of hope growing in me.

a gentle heart can pull others out of darkness

never underestimate the power of your softness

kindness flows from your fingertips

and brings light to those you touch

you are beauty in its purest form

look at how you made it through

the wars you thought would ruin you

WARRIOR

even when the moon is just a shadow of itself

it still has the force to change the tides of life

NEVER UNDERESTIMATE YOUR STRENGTH

i take a deep breath

though my heart is beating fast

i dress myself in strength

so that the heaviness can pass

I AM MORE THAN MY ANXIETY

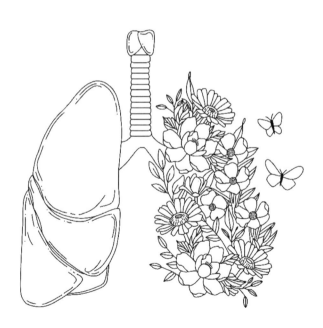

be kind to others for no reason

be the sun in their rainy season

RADIATE POSITIVITY

rise like the morning sun

and let the good be done

THE DAY IS WAITING FOR YOU

though the mountains seem impossible to climb

your strength will guide you one step at a time

FIND PEACE IN THE PROCESS

today I dragged my body from the bed

and let it feel the beauty of a life outside my head

SMALL STEPS OF COURAGE

here you are despite it all

standing when you thought you'd fall

YOUR STRENGTH IS UNDENIABLE

i know you have the strength

to fight for better days

i know your heart can bloom

once the darkness goes away

LET THE LIGHT FLOOD IN

heavy is the pain

yet she wears it like a feather

LION-HEARTED

fear not

for the heart that's always been deprived

can bloom once more and come alive

SPRING IS IN THE AIR

know that when you need it most

your strength will set your heart ablaze

and when the darkness slowly comes

the light will fill your days

you have struggled for so long

that your tender heart has hardened

but the tides are always changing

and your time is coming soon

so get ready for the clearing

place your heart out in the sun

and let its hardness thaw to joy

let the darkness be destroyed

you put pieces of your heart

in hands that hurt instead of held

this pain is going to change you

but your strength will remain

the ones who rise

from the remnants of destruction

can never be destroyed again

for now they have the wings to soar

if you carry the sun in your smile

every day will feel like summer

LET THE LIGHT POUR FROM YOU

the darkest parts of my soul

caught the light from your heat

you made the stars fiercely shine

through the nights i felt defeat

A NOTE TO MY STRENGTH

when the loneliness sets in

remember that inside you lives a universe

STAR CHILD

though starting over may seem hard

you have the strength to make it far

TIME WILL TAKE YOU WHERE YOUR HEART BELONGS

remember that the flower in its process of creation

needs the rain to help in growth and transformation

GOOD THINGS TAKE TIME

Final Words

It's time for us to part ways, and I want to thank you for arriving here with me at the end. I know it takes a lot of courage to unfasten your armour and allow my words to touch your heart. It's easier to keep everything locked inside. Still, there is an undeniable power that lies in vulnerability. Only through the people that share their stories with me can I hold my own pain and use it as inspiration to write these words and offer comfort to others.

The beauty of transparency is that it shows us the compassion and humanity that exists all around us, and I hope you give yourself a chance to experience it too.

As a writer, my job is to begin the story, but you, the reader, get to finish it. The only thing that matters to me is that you have found some relief in the journey and feel a little less alone in your troubles. If you haven't, that's also okay, and I hope you will give yourself the love and patience needed to heal your pain whenever you feel ready. I am rooting for you. May you never forget the power of light, for it is capable of piercing through the darkest night.